Seattle

Bruce,

Bonus points for
finding the mention
of fire-bellied
toads!

Karin

Seattle

A Downtown America Book

Karin Snelson

Dillon Press
New York

Maxwell Macmillan Canada
Toronto
Maxwell Macmillan International
New York Oxford Singapore Sydney

Dillon Press
Macmillan Publishing Company
866 Third Avenue
New York, NY 10022

Maxwell Macmillan Canada, Inc.
1200 Eglinton Avenue East
Suite 200
Don Mills, Ontario M3C 3N1

Macmillan Publishing Company is part of the Maxwell Communication Group of Companies.

First edition

Printed in the United States of America

10 9 8 7 6 5 4 3 2 1

Library of Congress Cataloging–in–Publication Data

Snelson, Karin.
    Seattle / by Karin Snelson.
       p.   cm. — (A Downtown America book)
    Includes index.
    Summary: Explores the city of Seattle, both past and present, describing its neighborhoods, attractions, festivals, and historic sites.
    ISBN 0–87518–509–6
    1. Seattle (Wash.)—Juvenile literature. [1. Seattle (Wash.)]
   1. Title. 11. Series.
F899.S457S64 1992
979.7'772—dc20   91–38232

ACKNOWLEDGMENTS
Special thanks to Murray Morgan, Bruce Taylor Hamilton and Larry Guldberg for their valuable suggestions.

Photographic Acknowledgments

Front Cover: James Blank
Back Cover: Karin Snelson

James Blank (2, 10, 29, 50); Karin Snelson (12, 14, 15, 16, 18, 23, 31, 36, 42, 44, 48, 53, 54); Major Marine Tours/Tillicum Village, Blake Island (20); Museum of History and Industry, Seattle (24, 26); Boeing Photos (30, 35); Generra Sportswear Company, Inc. (37); Seattle-King County Convention & Visitors Bureau (39, 40, 45, 47); The Kingdome (57)

Contents

Fast Facts about Seattle   6

1 A Watery City   11

2 Moving Mountains   21

3 Boeing and Beyond   33

4 Pockets of Seattle   41

5 An Endless Adventure   51

Places to Visit in Seattle   58

Seattle: A Historical Time Line   61

Index   62

City seal

Fast Facts about Seattle

Seattle: Emerald City, Gateway to the Pacific, Gateway to Gold

Location: Northwestern Washington State, on the eastern shore of Puget Sound, about 125 miles (201 kilometers) from the Pacific Ocean

Area: City, 92 square miles (238 square kilometers); consolidated metropolitan area, 6,103 square miles (15,807 square kilometers)

Population: (1990 official census figures): City, 516,259; consolidated metropolitan area, 1,972,961

Major Population Groups: Whites, blacks, Native Americans, and Asians (mainly Chinese, Filipino, Japanese, and Korean)

Altitude: 510 feet (155 meters) above sea level

Climate: Rainy. Average temperature is 41° F (5° C) in January, 66° F (19° C) in July; average annual precipitation, including rain and snow, is 34 inches (86 centimeters)

Founding Date: 1851, incorporated as a city in 1865

City Flag: Seattle is one of the only major American cities without a flag, because the city's officials never could decide what to put on it

City Seal: The profile of Chief Sealth, Seattle's namesake. The pine cones and whales at the bottom of the seal represent the natural beauty of the Northwest.

Form of Government: Mayor-council, with a four-year term for the mayor and the nine council members

Important Industries: Manufacturing (aircraft, cement, clay, fishing supplies, flour, metal products, textiles, food products), fishing, electronics, computer software development, tourism, technology, fashion

Festivals and Parades

January: Boat Show (Seattle Center, Kingdome)

February: Chinese New Year (International District)

March: Irish Heritage Week; Public Schools Fine Arts festivals

April: Things That Fly Fair; Seattle Center Easter Egg Hunt; KidsDay; International Children's Festival (Seattle Center)

May: Northwest Folklife Festival; Norwegian Constitution Day (Ballard); Opening Day of Yachting Season; Pike Place Market Festival; University District Street Fair

June: Harborfair; Fremont District Street Fair

July: Bon Odori (International District); Fratelli's Fireworks Festival; West Seattle Street Fair; SeaFair; Hispanic SeaFair Festival (Seward Park)

August: Black Community Festival; International District Street Fair; SeaFair Torchlight Parade; Seattle Boats Afloat Show

September: Bumbershoot; the Seattle Arts Festival

October: Haunted Houses (around Halloween); Pacific Northwest Arts Exposition

November: Boy Scout Show (Kingdome); Nutcracker (ballet) at the Seattle Opera House

December: Christmas Cruise; Christmas Around the World (Museum of History and Industry); Science Circus (Pacific Science Center)

For further information about festivals and parades, see agencies listed on page 60.

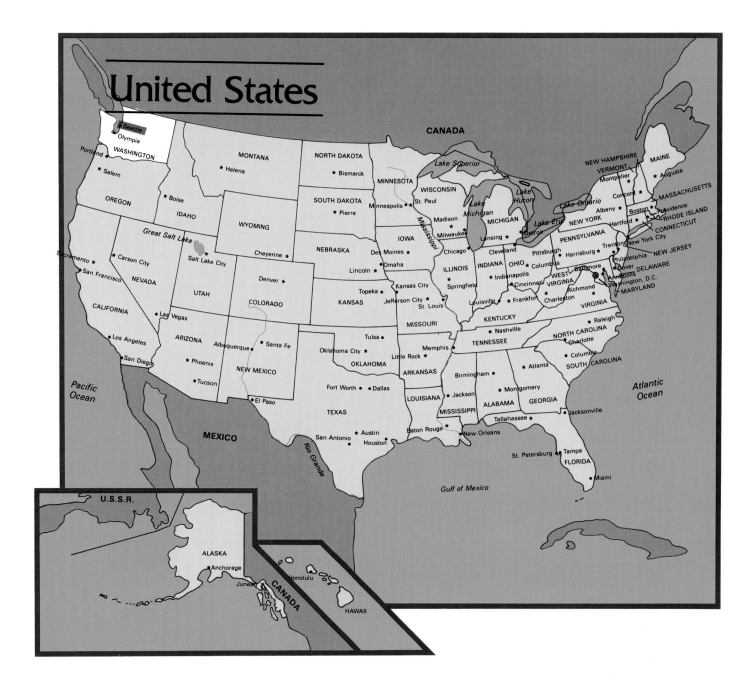

United States

Seattle

WASHINGTON
● Seattle

Seattle

Carkeek Park

Golden Gardens Park

Discovery Park

GREEN LAKE

Magnuson Park

Ravenna Park

⑦

⑤

INTERSTATE 99

INTERSTATE 5

⑧

Gas Works Park

LAKE UNION

The Arboretum

Myrtle Edwards Park

Volunteer Park

④

①

LAKE WASHINGTON

③

⑥

②

PUGET SOUND

⑨

Alki Beach

INTERSTATE 90

Points of Interest

① Seattle Center
② Pioneer Square
③ Pike Place Market
④ Capitol Hill
⑤ University of Washington
⑥ Seattle Art Museum
⑦ Woodland Park Zoo
⑧ Evergreen Point Bridge
⑨ Mercer Island Floating Bridge

Seward Park

Lincoln Park

INTERSTATE 509

INTERSTATE 99

0   1   miles   2   4   6
0   1   kilometers   5   10

1

A Watery City

Seattle is a city of surprising contrasts. Skylights in the sidewalks reveal a forgotten city underground, while across town a 607-foot Space Needle rises into the sky. Cobbled streets lead past quaint shops, as gleaming skyscrapers tower overhead. Ferry boats full of commuters from nearby islands pass giant cargo-carrying ocean freighters and dock at the bustling downtown terminal.

The surprising city of Seattle nestles in the northwestern corner of the United States. Home to over half a million people, it is the largest city in the Pacific Northwest. Seattle's setting, with the surrounding mountains, city lakes, and nearby ocean, makes it one of the most beautiful American cities.

Seattle is shaped like an hourglass—wide at the top and bottom

Lake Union, in the middle of Seattle, bustles with both commercial and pleasure boats.

The houseboats that line the shores of Seattle's Lake Union provide unique homes for some of the city's residents.

and pinched in the middle. Puget Sound forms a natural border to the west of the city, Lake Washington to the east. Beyond the Sound loom the Olympic Mountains, and in the east rise the majestic Cascades. The city's views of the snowy peaks are breathtaking, especially that of Mount Rainier, which is 14,410 feet (4,392 meters) high.

Downtown Seattle perches on the shores of Elliott Bay, a cove off Puget Sound, about 40 miles (64.5 kilometers) east of the Pacific Ocean. Truly a watery city, Seattle's waterfront location has shaped much of its history.

Native Americans were the first to discover the riches of Puget Sound. They lived there for almost 20,000 years before European settlers came with dreams of building a major port city. Thousands of prospectors bound for Alaska passed through the booming port in the gold rush days in the late 1890s. The next century saw the steady growth of trade across the waters of the Pacific.

Today, freighters from Asia load and unload millions of tons of cargo each year at Puget Sound ports. The Port of Seattle is linked to Lake Union, one of the city's freshwater lakes, by an unusual waterway system. All boats, whether on missions of business or pleasure, pass from Lake Union to the Sound through the Hiram M. Chittenden Locks.

Seattle's elevated monorail carries many people from Seattle Center to Westlake Mall.

Lake Union is located in the center of Seattle. Here, fishing boats, houseboats, and pleasure craft float next to freighters bound for nearby ports. Boats pass from Lake Union even farther east to Lake Washington, Seattle's largest lake, through the Montlake Cut, another part of the ship canal.

Spanning Lake Washington is one of the world's largest floating bridges, the Evergreen Point Floating

Wet air from the Pacific Ocean causes Seattle's rainy climate, which keeps the city's many parks green.

Bridge. This bridge and the southern I-90 freeway bridge slowly lead the city's traffic to the suburbs on Seattle's Eastside. Seattle and its suburbs make up Greater Seattle, which is part of King County.

Slicing through the eastern half of King County is the Cascade Range. According to a Native American legend, the Cascades were created when Ocean dug a trough in western Washington to keep his chil-

dren, Cloud and Rain, at home. The dirt made a mighty wall of mountains, and the trough became Puget Sound.

The Cascades contribute greatly to Seattle's wet climate. The mountains trap the wet air from the Pacific Ocean, blanketing the city in clouds three-fourths of the year. The enormous amount of rainfall has helped create luxurious rain forests filled with giant, dripping ferns and blankets of moss.

"The rain in Spain falls mainly in Seattle," proclaims a popular T-shirt slogan. While some people may get tired of the mist, the moist climate does keep the parks and gardens green year-round. Seattle's park sys-

The city continues to grow as more and more people discover the joys of living in Seattle.

tem covers more than 3,800 acres (1,540 hectares), and the overall landscape is so green that some people call Seattle the Emerald City. The Washington Park Arboretum, Lincoln Park, Discovery Park, Gas Works Park and Volunteer Park are among the best known of the city's 140 different parks. Visitors to Seattle's parks can hike, bike, swim, windsurf, and simply enjoy the outdoors.

To visitors from huge, busy cities like New York or Los Angeles, Seattle has a laid back, relaxing atmosphere. About 50,000 people discover the city's appeal each year and decide to make Seattle their home. These newcomers bring their skills to the city and help create new

jobs. For years, many Seattleites worked for Boeing, the nation's leader in aircraft manufacturing. Today, the city is breaking ground in other areas as well, such as international trade, computer software production, electronics, biotechnology, and fashion.

With the increase in population, Seattle has had to adapt. Modern urban problems are disturbing the small-town feeling that attracted so many people to the city. Overcrowding is causing traffic jams, and new construction is tearing up streets. There is not enough low-income housing for the growing population, and the crime rate is rising.

To meet Seattle's growing needs,

restaurants, hotels, shopping centers, and skyscrapers are springing up all over the city. A new convention center opened in 1988, built above 12 freeway lanes. New high-rises, such as the 76-story Columbia Seafirst Center, tower above the city.

Whether you are admiring the shiny new skyscrapers or visiting historic spots like Pioneer Square, Seattle is an exciting place to discover and explore. The watery city of the Pacific Northwest has a new and changing face. But like Seattle's early pioneers, today's citizens are meeting the future's challenges head-on.

New skyscrapers, such as the tall black Columbia Seafirst Center, now rise high above Smith Tower (left), which until 1939 was the tallest building west of Chicago, Illinois!

2

Moving Mountains

The Salish Indians native to the shores of Puget Sound were a peaceful fishing community. Their land was bountiful. The Sound was a fine location for fishing and canoeing, the forests supplied building materials, and the wild animals provided hides for the fur trade.

These riches attracted white European explorers. Soon adventurers from England, Russia, Spain, and the East Coast of America were making their way to the shores of the Sound. Many people were interested in claiming the rich land for their country, but in 1846 the area that is now Washington State became American territory.

In 1851, a group of settlers from Illinois, led by Arthur Denny, landed on the beach in what is now West Seattle. The settlers called the area

Visitors to Tillicum Village on nearby Blake Island can experience Native American culture in a traditional longhouse.

New York-Alki, which means "New York by-and-by" in the language of the region's Native Americans. These newcomers hoped that, by-and-by, their town would become as important a port as New York. The open shoreline of New York-Alki offered little protection from the winds and rain, and the people endured hard winters. Soon the settlers moved inland, to sheltered Elliott Bay.

The Salish and other Native American groups welcomed the newcomers, who brought tools, liquor, and blankets. Many of them helped the settlers get started in their new home. One man in particular, a Suquamish tribe leader named Sealth, was a good friend to the settlers. They decided to name their new community after the friendly chief. Because the name Sealth was hard to pronounce, the town became known as Seattle.

Despite a peaceful beginning, tension soon grew between the Salish and the settlers. Along with supplies, the whites brought disease, a new religion, and the idea of private property. The Salish did not believe that anyone owned the land—they had always shared it among their people. As they saw more and more settlers arriving from the East, they began to feel threatened. As they suspected, the white people soon told them that they wanted the land the Indians had lived on for centuries. The Indians would be paid for their land and placed on reservations, tracts of land set aside by the U.S. government.

The Salish chose to fight rather than give up their homeland. They planned an all-out attack on the settlers. On January 26, 1856, the Battle of Seattle began. The U.S. military, however, was ready for the attack. A navy ship in the bay successfully defended the town from what could have been a bloody massacre. The area now belonged entirely to the settlers.

Lumber was Seattle's first major industry. Preparing logs to sell as lumber was hard work. To bring the huge logs to the sawmill, workers dragged them down Seattle's steep hills, along a cleared stretch of land called Skid Row. From that name

A bust of Sealth, the Suquamish Indian leader who befriended Arthur Denny and his settlers and after whom Seattle is named.

Residents of Seattle begin to rebuild their city shortly after the fire of 1889.

comes the term Skid Row, meaning an area in a rough part of town or a place for people who are down on their luck.

As loggers, shipbuilders, and fishermen moved in, Seattle began to grow. Very few women came to the rough town, however, until a man named Asa Mercer had an idea. Collecting money from Seattle's unmarried men, Mercer traveled to the East Coast. There he persuaded several young women to go to Seattle to find husbands. Because there were no planes or trains to transport the women quickly, the "Mercer Girls" took a long journey by ship around the tip of South America to arrive at the port of Seattle.

The most exciting event in Seattle after the arrival of the women was the coming of the railroad. In the 1880s, the trains brought thousands of people from the East who were looking for a new life. In one decade, the town's population rose from 3,300 to 43,000. New businesses, parks, and schools appeared everywhere. The streets bustled with activity as horse-drawn carriages rolled by the saloons and stores.

This success came to a sudden halt when, on June 6, 1889, a huge fire destroyed the city. A boy in a woodwork shop had been heating a pot of glue over a gasoline stove when the glue boiled over, igniting the wood shavings scattered on the floor. The blaze spread out of control, and 25 city blocks burned to the ground.

Within days, a city of tents appeared, and the citizens turned the disastrous fire into an opportunity to rethink their city plans. Seattle's streets had been too narrow, and drainage had been poor. Each day, the high tide washing up from the shores of Elliott Bay had filled the streets with mud and water, turning toilets into spouting geysers.

The townspeople solved the drainage problem by raising the street level 9 feet (2.74 meters).

Forceful jets of water were used to wash away some of the hills that once made up Seattle's downtown area.

They built their new city directly on top of the old town. Today, Seattle's "forgotten city" can be seen on the Underground Tour, in the old part of town called Pioneer Square. Down some rickety stairs lie abandoned shops, bank safes, and a few rats.

Thick purple blocks of glass in the sidewalks serve as skylights to the passageways underground.

The new construction that followed the 1889 fire helped prepare Seattle for its next growth spurt. The 1897 Klondike gold rush in Alaska brought crowds of people through the city on their way to and from the gold mines. Saloons and restaurants tripled in number, and business flourished as Seattle became known as the Gateway to Gold.

The city was growing fast. Since developers wanted to build more houses and roads, some of Seattle's steep hills would have to be flattened. They were so steep that in the early 1900s members of the Seattle Symphony had to rig a pulley to haul their heavy instruments to the top. Traveling cellos and tubas surprised more than a few newcomers to the city!

In 1906, developers decided to flatten huge Denny Hill. Hotels, houses, and churches standing on 62 city blocks were destroyed, and work-ers pumped millions of gallons of water through powerful hoses to wash the dirt into Elliott Bay. Work on the project continued off and on for 24 years.

Seattle was taking shape, and by 1909 was home to 237,000 citizens. The Alaska-Yukon-Pacific Exposi-tion, a huge fair, brought even more people to the area. The fair was cre-ated to spotlight Seattle's growing trade with Alaska, California, and Asia.

Seattle drew national attention a decade later as the site of the first general strike ever held in the United States. The strike started in the shipyards, when shipbuilders protested a cut in their wages. Soon metalworkers, carpenters, and other workers joined the strike until 110 unions of all kinds were involved.

On February 6, 1919, all work stopped—even the schools and banks closed. One striker said it was so quiet you could hear grass grow. A week later, the strike ended. Although they didn't receive a pay raise, the 60,000 workers felt their point had been made, and they began to work again.

The strike made national news, but it didn't hurt Seattle or its most important business, the aircraft-building company called Boeing. In the early 1920s the Boeing Company received its first U.S. government order to build military planes. By the fall of 1941, Boeing was the largest company in the Northwest.

The World War II years were a time of growth and prosperity for Seattle, thanks to Boeing and the shipbuilding industry. But they were a time of pain for one part of the city's population, the Japanese Americans.

After the Japanese bombed Pearl Harbor on December 7, 1941, some groups of Americans viewed Japanese Americans with fear and suspicion. Soon a government order forced Japanese Americans in the western United States to leave their homes. Seattle's 7,000 Japanese-Americans were sent to internment camps in California, Idaho, and other western states.

When the war ended, some of the Japanese Americans came back.

Many of them had lost their homes and jobs, and many were bitter about their harsh treatment. Today, over 20,000 Japanese Americans continue to call Seattle home, and make valuable contributions to the city's economic and cultural life.

Twenty years after the events of World War II, a better chapter in Seattle's history opened with the 1962 World's Fair. Also known as the Century 21 Exposition, this event changed Seattle forever. The Seattle Center, the Opera House, a theater, a sports coliseum, the Pacific Science Center, and a speedy new monorail were all built in record time for the event. The most famous structure built for the fair was the Space Needle. The strangely shaped, 607-foot-

One of the most famous sites in Seattle, the Space Needle was built for the 1962 World's Fair.

tall (185 meters) Needle has become one of Seattle's best-known landmarks.

The 1990 Goodwill Games put Seattle in the world spotlight again. The games were advertised as the "most prestigious multisport competition in the United States for the next decade." This 17-day competition attracted 2,500 athletes from more than 50 countries. The Goodwill Arts Festival brought the Soviet Union's Bolshoi Ballet and many exhibits of Soviet art to Seattle. A large trade exhibition also highlighted the occasion.

Since the World's Fair, Seattle has grown rapidly. Today, the city's citizens have united to control the city's growth. They have passed laws limiting the height and size of office buildings in the downtown area. They also have fought to protect the city's historic sections. When developers wanted to tear down the Pike Place Market in the 1960s, people protested loudly. Finally, in 1971, the market was listed and protected by the National Register of Historic Places.

Seattle's city planners are taking steps to relieve the city's increasing traffic problems. A new freeway bridge spans Lake Washington, and an underground bus system downtown handles 25 percent of the rush-hour traffic. A gallery of murals and sculptures line this underground bus tunnel.

Judging from the city's past, the

Soviet sailors in town for the 1990 Goodwill Games.

people of Seattle will find ways to overcome their current challenges. Seattleites have shown they will move mountains if necessary to support their city's growth while preserving its heritage, its relaxed atmosphere, and its natural beauty.

A Boeing 767 soars over the mountains outside Seattle.

3

Boeing and Beyond

Seattle has come a long way from its early frontier days. The lumber industry that used to be the town's most important business was nudged aside by the tourist, electronics, computer software and, most important, aircraft manufacturing industries.

The Boeing Company, which manufactures commercial jets, military equipment, and aerospace products, is the largest exporter of aircraft equipment in the United States.

One in ten Seattleites works for Boeing, and the company has been called the pulse of Seattle.

When Boeing prospers, so does Seattle. When the company's business slows down, so does the city. Some people say, "Every time Boeing sneezes, Seattle comes down with a cold." As recently as 1989, the national newspapers called a Boeing strike a blow to Seattle's economy.

The close relationship between

Boeing and its headquarters city began in 1916, when William Boeing, a young millionaire, decided to construct planes in Seattle. The business prospered as the United States prepared to enter World War I. Workers came to Seattle by the hundreds to help the company build military aircraft. By the time the government needed Boeing again, to build aircraft for World War II, the business was a giant. In only a few decades, 50,000 aerospace mechanics and engineers had joined the company.

When World War II ended, Boeing ran into trouble. The country no longer needed wartime aircraft. To survive, Boeing turned its energies to peacetime projects. In 1956, the first 707 passenger plane was built. This airplane was a huge success, and it paved the way for the 727, the 737, the 747 jumbo jet, and the 767. Today, some of Boeing's first aircraft designs can be seen at the Museum of Flight as well as at the Museum of History and Industry.

When Boeing experienced hard times, Seattleites realized they could not continue to rely on just one company. They turned to the Port of Seattle. The deep waters of Seattle's harbor connect with the Pacific Ocean, making the Port of Seattle the perfect location for trading ships from Asia and Alaska.

Today, Seattle is one of the world's largest container ports. Containers are the huge ocean freighter boxes that carry cargo. They are

Seattle's main industry, the Boeing Company employs more people than any other business.

Once a busy dock for cargo-carrying ships, the Waterfront is now lined with parks, shops, and fish and chip stands.

With companies like Generra setting up headquarters in Seattle, the city is a growing center in the fashion industry.

stacked on ships, and can also be transported by trains or trucks. The Port of Seattle does business with more than 100 countries, handling $25 billion in trade each year. One out of every five jobs in Seattle depends on international trade. The big trading ships load and unload their cargo at Harbor Island, the largest man-made island in the world. Seattle sends airplanes, logs, corn, cattle hides, vehicles, and lumber to customers around the world.

One third of all clothing and textile imports in the United States also pass through the Port of Seattle. Thousands of Asian clothing factories are located across the Pacific. That activity has encouraged fashion companies such as Generra, International News, and Code Bleu to make Seattle their home.

Another rapidly growing industry in Seattle is science research. The University of Washington and the Fred Hutchinson Cancer Research Center are known internationally for research in biology and medicine.

Electronics and computer software development are also becoming increasingly important to Seattle's economy. Computer products are produced in a series of business parks known as Technology Corridor. This corridor is on the Eastside, the suburban area across from Seattle over Lake Washington. Here, companies such as Microsoft (computer software) and Advanced Technology Laboratories (medical equipment) work to keep pace with an ever-changing market.

Tourism is another major source of income for Seattle. Each year in King County, tourism brings in about a billion dollars and supports some 30,000 jobs. The construction of the new Washington State Convention and Trade Center in 1988 encouraged tourism by bringing trade shows and business conferences to the city.

Expanding industries are creat-

Many products imported into the Port of Seattle are bought and sold in the shops and markets on the piers of Elliott Bay.

ing new jobs and a new variety of job opportunities in Seattle. No longer a one-company town, Seattle today is building a more secure economy by relying on the strengths of many industries.

The giant dragon mural in Hing Hay Park brightens a corner of the colorful International District.

4

Pockets of Seattle

Seattle is like a cluster of small villages. A city explorer never has to go far before stumbling upon a new neighborhood, completely different from the one before.

Downtown Seattle has far more office than living space, but many people like to live in the heart of the city anyway. Some live in condominiums or apartments near the Pike Place Market, others in studios above historic Pioneer Square. Living downtown saves hours of fighting traffic to get to work. Seattle's bus system transports people all over the city, and within a downtown area people can ride the buses free between 4:00 A.M. and 9:00 P.M.

One of Seattle's most lively and interesting downtown neighborhoods is the International District, or Chinatown. The streets here bustle

with activity, especially during the weekends when families shop in the area's small stores, and the many Japanese, Chinese, Korean, and Vietnamese restaurants fill the air with delicious smells. Surprises, such as a dusty toy shop, a pet store filled with fire-bellied toads, a noodle house, or a pagoda-shaped telephone booth appear around every corner.

People from China, the Philippines, Japan, Korea, Vietnam, Cambodia, Laos, and other Asian countries have made their homes here and in other areas of the city. The Japanese influence on Seattle becomes obvious as soon as you go to the airport. Since Japan is one of Seattle's biggest international trade partners, the signs and recordings

A townhouse in the popular Capitol Hill district.

here are in Japanese as well as English. Many signs at Seattle's major hotels and tourist spots are also in both languages.

Just outside of the downtown area is one of Seattle's busiest neighborhoods, Capitol Hill. The area was named in Seattle's early days, when the city was being considered as the site for Washington's state capital. Eventually, Olympia was chosen instead, but the name stuck.

Today, Capitol Hill is a large, heavily populated community. It is a strange mixture of different kinds of people and different styles of homes, from punk rockers to retirees, from fine old mansions to run-down shacks painted with graffiti. The main area of stores and restaurants is a street called Broadway, where trendy restaurants and boutiques stand beside fast-food outlets and secondhand shops.

The recreational center of Capitol Hill is Volunteer Park. The park houses the original Seattle Art Museum building (now an Asian art exhibit center), and a historic conservatory (greenhouse) full of unusual plants.

South of Capitol Hill is one of Seattle's oldest neighborhoods, the Central Area. A large percentage of the city's black population lives here. Although parts of the Central Area are run-down, much of it is being rebuilt and improved with pride.

Poverty and racial prejudice have been problems for many Seat-

Decorated with balloons, *Waiting for the Interurban* greets travelers at the north end of the Fremont Bridge.

tleites since World War II. It has been especially difficult for blacks in the city to gain a political voice and to get fair housing and job opportunities. In 1972, the city tried to encourage integration and to improve education for black children by starting a program of school busing. In 1989, busing was still a major issue for Seattle's voters and political candidates running for mayor. That year, Seattle elected Norm Rice to office, making him the city's first black mayor.

North of the Central Area is the ever-changing University District. As its name implies, the district surrounds the University of Washington, one of the largest and most respected universities in the Northwest. The main street of the "U. District" is University Way NE, which everyone calls "The Ave." Coffeehouses, theaters, stores, and many kinds of ethnic restaurants line this busy street.

West of the university is a small funky neighborhood known as Fremont. This colorful district is separated from the downtown area and Queen Anne Hill by the ship canal and Lake Union. At the northeast end of the brightly painted Fremont Bridge is a famous sculpture called

Two of the inhabitants of the Woodland Park Zoo.

Waiting for the Interurban. Created by artist Richard Beyer, it is a life-sized sculpture of people and a dog waiting for a trolley. Almost every day, for any and every occasion, people dress the statues in old clothes and decorate the sculpture with balloons and signs.

One unusual Fremont resident is the giant Fremont Troll that lurks under the Aurora Bridge, rolling its eyes and clasping an unlucky Volkswagen bug in its giant fist. At Halloween, people in costumes dance under the bridge and bring their jack-o'-lanterns to display on the troll.

Fremont is also full of unique stores, including Archie McPhee & Company, a store full of fascinating toys that glow in the dark, squeak, walk, or just entertain. Many of the area's stores participate in the festive and colorful Fremont Sunday Market, which is held every weekend, rain or shine.

On the northern border of Fremont is the Woodland Park Zoo. Here, many animals wander freely within large fenced areas. The Great Ape House, Monkey Island, and the Snake House contain hundreds of exotic animals. Zoo-animal babies needing special care are kept in the Children's Zoo. Next to the Children's Zoo is Poncho Theater, which presents plays, "Meet the Animals" programs, lectures, and films for young people.

Just northeast of the zoo is

The many drawbridges found throughout Seattle lift to let boats pass in and out of the city's many waterways.

Green Lake and the community named after it. Throughout the year people roller-skate, bike, jog, and walk around the lake or play on the area's softball fields and tennis courts. In the summer, the Green Lake community offers swimming, sailing, and basking in the sun. During a celebration called SeaFair, Seattleites participating in the Milk Carton Derby fill the lake with odd shapes and ships made out of old milk cartons. At Christmastime, people line the sidewalk around the lake with luminarios (candles in paper bags) and sing carols.

Farther west lies Puget Sound and Seattle's shoreside neighborhoods. Just east of a beautiful strip of beach called Shilshole and Golden Gardens Park area is the neighborhood of Ballard. It was formerly a fishing community. Today, many of Ballard's residents are descendants of Scandinavian immigrants, who came to the area to work as lumbermen and fishermen. Even today, Seattle has the nation's largest number of halibut and salmon fishing boats.

Boats wait to be raised to the next level in the Ballard Locks.

At Ballard's Hiram M. Chittenden Locks, boats of all shapes and sizes make their way to and from the inland waters of Lake Union and the saltwater of Puget Sound. The lake and the Sound are all at different water levels, and the Sound's level changes as the tides come in and out. The locks raise or lower the boats, depending on where they're heading.

Boats aren't the only things that pass through the locks. From June to October, visitors can view migrating fish through an underground window or from overhead walkways. Each year, 113 million salmon and trout swim up the locks' 21-step fish ladder to get to their spawning ground.

Across Lake Washington is the Eastside, where the growing suburbs of Bellevue, Issaquah, Kirkland, Redmond and Mercer Island form what some developers call "Pugetopolis." This odd word comes from the name Puget Sound and *polis*, the Greek word meaning city. Some of Seattle's suburbs are islands. From areas such as Vashon and Bainbridge Island, commuters ride a ferry to get to work.

From suburb to city, Seattle offers a great variety of places to live. Whether Seattleites prefer life in the fast lane of downtown or the slow pace of Ballard, their city offers the choice.

5

An Endless Adventure

A wonderful place to start exploring Seattle is down by the salty-smelling docks of Elliott Bay. In Seattle's early days, all ships coming to Elliott Bay docked near Yesler's Wharf, now called just the Waterfront.

Today, you won't find big trading ships here. Instead, the boats at the docks more likely will be harbor-tour boats and ferries. On these piers, you can eat fish-and-chips or poke around in stores that sell Seattle T-shirts and other keepsakes.

One unusual store is called Ye Olde Curiosity Shop. The shop has a mummy, strange shrunken heads, and two-headed calf embryos, as well as an enormous selection of souvenirs.

Down the street are the huge, dome-shaped Omnidome Theater

The restaurants and shops of Seattle's waterfront bustle with excitement at any time of the year.

and the Seattle Aquarium. Inside the aquarium, you walk beneath a replica of a great white shark on your way past a coral reef to the Touch Tank. Here, you can touch starfish, feather-duster worms, and sea anemones. The vast Underwater Dome is home to darting fish, sharks, and a giant Pacific octopus.

Beyond the aquarium is the Washington State Ferry Terminal, used by many commuters and tourists. A ferry ride is an adventure, even if you only go to nearby Winslow and back. Many people take the trip just to see the remarkable views of the city skyline and the mountains or to feel the cool, salty ocean breezes.

Up the hill from Seattle's waterfront is the Pike Place Market. The market is a feast for the senses. Colorful flower, fruit, and vegetable stands form a winding maze of streets. Puppeteers and street musicians entertain the onlookers. Delicious smells rise from dozens of international restaurants, food stands, and bakeries.

Within walking distance of the market is Seattle's most historic corner, Pioneer Square. Here, it's easy to imagine the carriages, saloons, and gold diggers of the historic Northwest. Signs hanging outside the brick buildings still read ROOMS 75¢ or COFFEE 5¢ in memory of the past.

Seattle's famous Underground

Tour at Pioneer Square leads curious people through the old city, buried after the fire of 1889. "Dirt! Corruption! Sewers! Scandal!" is the advertisement that tour guides use to encourage people to explore the colorful history.

A short walk north toward the center of downtown Seattle is Westlake Mall. Here, designer shops and large department stores line polished Fifth Avenue. At Christmastime, the whole area is lighted beautifully and a large carousel twirls to festive music.

If you board the monorail that leaves from the mall, a 90-second ride will take you to one of the most exciting places in the city, the Seat-

A fishmonger at Pike Place Market entertains onlookers as he sells the fresh daily catch.

tle Center. This recreational center is always easy to find, because here the Space Needle towers above the skyline.

The Space Needle would stand out even if it weren't so tall. It looks like something out of a science-fiction movie. The Needle has a revolving restaurant near the top. It also has a round observation deck, which offers a spectacular view of the whole city. A machine on the viewing deck will flatten a penny and stamp it with a picture of the Needle and the Olympic Range.

From the southern side of the viewing deck, you can see the city's other major landmark, the Kingdome stadium. Built in 1976, the King-dome has the world's largest self-supporting concrete roof. It is the home stadium for two of Seattle's four professional sports teams, the Seattle Seahawks (football) and the Mariners (baseball). The Kingdome also houses trade shows, industrial shows, concerts, circuses, and other special events.

Once you've enjoyed the view from the top of the Space Needle, there are many attractions yet to explore in the Seattle Center. Here you will find the Pacific Science Center, which has many fun exhibits. At a place called Kids Works, there is a giant bubble-making machine, and you can experiment with a television monitor at

At historic Pioneer Square, visitors can get a taste of life during the gold rush and take a tour of the underground ruins of the old city.

the video stage. In the Body Works area, skeletons dance and hands-on exhibits show how the human body works. The Science Playground has a space-simulator machine that spins you around and turns you upside down. In the Science of Sports area, rats play basketball and exhibits explain why curve balls curve.

Also in the center are a planetarium, laser fantasy music and light shows, and the IMAX movie theater with its 3 1/2 story screen. The Seattle Center's Children's Museum is a playground with a child-sized neighborhood, including a post office, a school, a bank and a grocery store. Here, young people can learn what it's like to be an active part of a community.

This idea of community is what makes Seattle unique. No matter how fast the town grows, it always seems to stay friendly and relaxed. From its beginning, the community has treasured these qualities and has fought to protect them.

This is the spirit that rebuilt the city after the fire of 1889 and fought to control its growth over 100 years later. Community pride is one of Seattle's main strengths. And it is this pride that will carry the changing city successfully through the 1990s and beyond.

The enormous Kingdome, the home of the Seattle Seahawks and the Seattle Mariners, backed by the snowy Olympic Range.

Places to Visit in Seattle

The Seattle Aquarium
Pier 59, Waterfront Park
(206) 386-4320

Archie McPhee & Company
3510 Stone Way North, Fremont
(206) 545-8344
A store jammed with unusual toys and gifts

The Seattle Art Museum
First Avenue and University (downtown)
(206) 625-8900

Thomas Burke Memorial Washington State Museum
University of Washington campus
(206) 543-5590
Natural history as well as history of the northwestern United States

Seattle Center
305 Harrison Street
(206) 684-8582

Seattle Children's Museum
Seattle Center House
(206) 441-1768

Elliott Bay Book Company
First Avenue and South Main (Pioneer Square)
(206) 624-6600

Hiram M. Chittenden Locks
(Ballard Locks)
3015 NW 54th
(206) 783-7059 (Visitor's Center)

IMAX Theater
Pacific Science Center,
Seattle Center
(206) 443-4629

Kingdome Stadium
201 South King Street
(206) 296-3111 (Ticket Office)

Klondike Gold Rush
National Historic Park
117 S. Main Street
(206) 553-7220

Museum of Flight
9404 East Marginal Way South
Exit I-5 South at #158 (Tukwila)
(206) 764-5720

Museum of History and Industry
2700 24th Avenue East, Montlake
(206) 324-1125

Nordic Heritage Museum
3014 NW 67th Street
(206) 789-5707

Pacific Science Center
200 Second Avenue North (Seattle
Center)
(206) 443-2880

Tillicum Village and Tours, Inc.
2200 Sixth Avenue, Suite 804
(206) 443-1244
Native American longhouse on Blake Island

Underground Tour
610 First Avenue (Pioneer Square)
(206) 682-1511

Washington State Ferries
Pier 52, Colman Dock
(206) 464-6400

Wing Luke Asian Museum
407 Seventh Avenue South
(206) 623-5124
An Asian history museum in the International District

Woodland Park Zoo
5500 Phinney Avenue North
(206) 684-4800

Additional information can be obtained from:
Greater Seattle Chamber of Commerce
600 University Street,
Suite 1200
One Union Square Building,
12th Floor
Seattle, WA 98101
(206) 389-7200

Seattle King County Convention and Visitors Bureau
520 Pike Street, Suite 1300
Seattle, WA 98101
(206) 461-5840

Seattle: A Historical Time Line

1792 British Captain James Vancouver discovers Puget Sound

1841 Lieutenant Charles Wilkes surveys Puget Sound and names Elliott Bay

1851 First white people land at Alki Point

1852 Settlement moves to Elliott Bay

1853 Washington Territory formed

1856 The Battle of Seattle is fought

1861 University of Washington founded

1865 Seattle is incorporated as a city on January 18

1875 Steamship service begins between Seattle and San Francisco

1883 Women win the right to vote in Seattle

1886 Anti-Chinese riots surface, and Americans force the Chinese out of the city

1889 The Great Seattle Fire of June 6 destroys the city; Washington becomes a state

1893 The first transcontinental railroad, the Great Northern, reaches Seattle

1897 Klondike gold rush in Alaska brings many people through the Seattle area

1903 Seattle Symphony Orchestra is founded

1916 The Boeing Company is established

1917 The Hiram M. Chittenden Locks and Lake Washington Ship Canal open

1919 First labor strike in U.S. history begins in Seattle

1940 Evergreen Point Floating Bridge opens

1962 World's Fair, the Century 21 Exposition, opens at the Seattle Center

1970–1971 Boeing loses a major contract, and the city's economy slumps

1988 Washington State Convention and Trade Center built

1989 Washington State's Centennial (100th Anniversary of Washington's Statehood); first black mayor, Norm Rice, elected to office; Seattle citizens vote to curb downtown growth

1990 The Goodwill Games put Seattle in the world spotlight; Metro bus tunnel opens downtown

1991 Seattle Art Museum opens downtown

Index

aircraft, 33, 34
Alaska-Yukon-Pacific Exposition, 27
Aurora Bridge, 46

Bainbridge Island, 15, 49
Ballard, 48-49
Battle of Seattle, 23
Bellevue, 49
Beyer, Richard, 46
Boeing Company, 17, 28, 33-34
Boeing, William, 34
Bolshoi Ballet, 30

Capitol Hill, 43
Cascades, 13, 15, 16
Central Area, 43
Century 21 Exposition (1962 World's Fair), 29, 30
climate, 16
Columbia Seafirst Center, 19
computer software, 17, 33, 38

Denny, Arthur, 21
Denny Hill, 27
Discovery Park, 17

Eastside, 15, 38, 49
economy, 33-34, 37-39
electronics, 17, 33, 38
Elliott Bay, 13, 22, 25, 27, 51
ethnic groups, 41-43
European explorers, 21
Evergreen Point Floating Bridge, 14-15

fashion, 17, 38
"forgotten city," 26
fire of 1889, 25, 26, 53,56
Fremont, 45-46
Fremont Bridge, 45
Fremont Troll, 46

Gas Works Park, 17
Goodwill Arts Festival, 30
Goodwill Games (1990), 30
Green Lake, 46-48

Harbor Island, 37
Hiram M. Chittenden Locks, 13, 49

Indian reservations, 22-23
International District (Chinatown), 41
internment camps, 28
Issaquah, 49

Japanese, 42-43
Japanese Americans, 28, 29, 41-43

King County, 15, 38
Kingdome stadium, 55
Kirkland, 49
Klondike gold rush, 13, 26-27

Lake Union, 13, 14, 45, 49
Lake Washington, 13, 14, 30, 38
Lincoln Park, 17
lumber, 23, 33

Mercer, Asa, 24
Mercer Girls, 25
Mercer Island, 49
Montlake Cut, 14
Mount Rainier, 13
Museum of Flight, 34
Museum of History and Industry, 34

Native Americans, 13, 22
New York-Alki, 22

Olympic Mountains, 13
Omnidome Theater, 51
Opera House, 29

Pacific Ocean, 13, 16, 34
Pacific Science Center, 29, 55-56
Pike Place Market, 30, 41, 52
Pioneer Square, 19, 26, 41, 52, 53
population, 11, 17, 25, 41-44
Port of Seattle, 13, 34, 38
Puget Sound, 13, 16, 21, 48, 49

rain forests, 11, 16
Redmond, 49
Rice, Norm, 44

Salish Indians, 21, 22, 23
science research, 38
SeaFair, 47
Sealth, 22

Seattle Aquarium, 52
Seattle Art Museum, 43
Seattle Center, 29, 54-55
settlers, 21, 22, 23
shipping, 34
shipyards, 27
Skid Row, 23-24
Space Needle, 11, 29-30, 55
strike, 27-28

Technology Corridor, 38
tourism, 33, 38
trade, 13, 17, 27, 34, 37-38

University District, 45

Vashon, 49
Volunteer Park, 17, 43

Waiting for the Interurban, 45-46
Washington State Convention and Trade Center,
    38
Waterfront, 51
West Seattle, 21
Westlake Mall, 53
Woodland Park Zoo, 46
World War I, 34
World War II, 28, 34
Yesler's Wharf, 51

About the Author

Karin Snelson is a writer and designer for a Seattle toy company. Before moving to Seattle, she edited children's books for Dillon Press in Minneapolis.